C000181689

FAMOUS LAST TURDS

HARRY KANE & KEVIN SPENDER

Old St PUBLISHING

Old Street Publishing Ltd, 28-32 Boweling Green Lane,
London EC1R 0BJ, UK
www.oldstreetpublishing.co.uk

ISBN-13: 978-1-905847-60-0

10 9 8 7 6 5 4 3 2 1

A CIP catalogue record for this book is available from the British
Library.

Printed in Singapore by SC (Sang Choy) International Pte Ltd

*"You can tell a lot about a man
from what he leaves in the pan"*
Jonathan Swift

KING ARTHUR

MARILYN MONROE

(THE TURD FORMERLY KNOWN AS)
PRINCE

SNOOPY

ISAMBARD
KINGDOM BRUNEL

HANNIBAL

COLONEL SANDERS

NEIL ARMSTRONG

BILL GATES

DAVID BLAINE

PARIS HILTON

SIMON COWELL

GODZILLA

TINTIN

STEVIE WONDER

HARRY POTTER

JOAN OF ARC

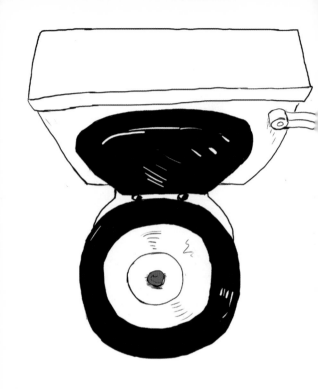

TIGER WOODS

JACK THE RIPPER

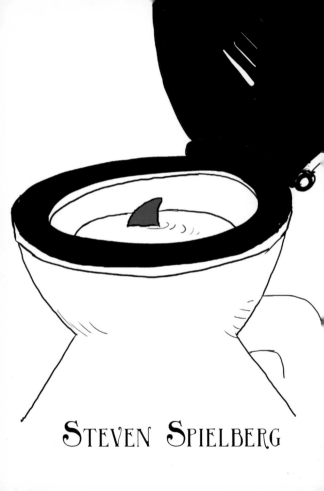

STEVEN SPIELBERG

THE TERMINATOR

ANDY McNAB

THE INCREDIBLE HULK

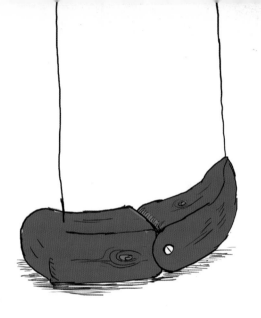

PINOCCHIO

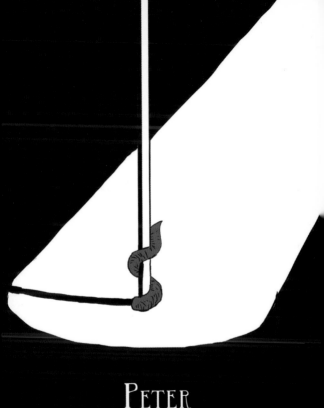

PETER
STRINGFELLOW

Sigmund Freud

Erno Rubik

Mother
Teresa

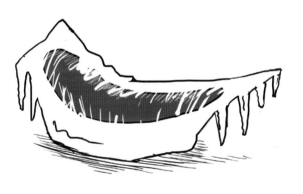

Scott
of the Antarctic

Frodo Baggins

HUGH HEFNER

JAMES DYSON

GEORGE FOREMAN

Bruce Willis

EVEL KNIEVEL

NORMAN
SCHWARZKOPF

JOHN & YOKO

DORIAN GRAY

E.T.

DAVID HASSELHOFF

URI GELLER

THE FANTASTIC FOUR

KATE WINSLET &
LEONARDO DICAPRIO

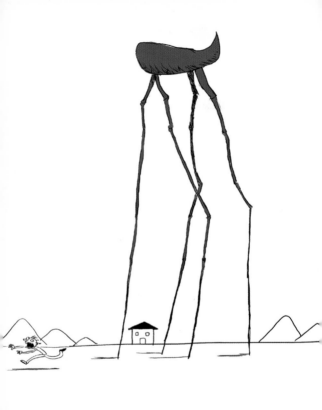

SALVADOR DALI

COUNT DRACULA

INDIANA JONES

DAMIEN HIRST

JESUS

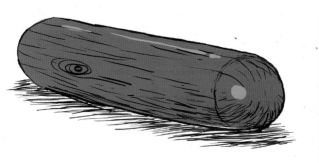

KEANU REEVES

LENIN

BANKSY

OPTIMUS PRIME

H.R.H.
The Queen

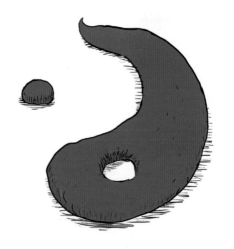

CONFUCIUS

CAPTAIN KIRK

THE INVISIBLE MAN

GEORGE W. BUSH

THE A-TEAM

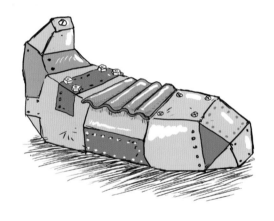

Margaret
Thatcher

SPIDERMAN

PAUL DANIELS
& DEBBIE McGEE

SUPERMAN

DARTH VADER

JULIUS CAESAR

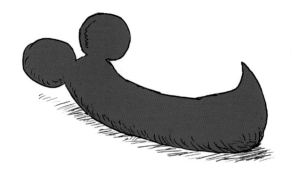

WALT DISNEY

TUTANKHAMUN

PETER PAN

STANLEY KUBRICK

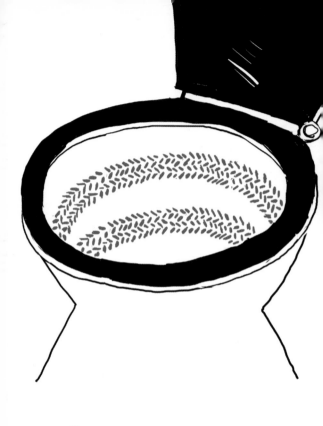

LEWIS HAMILTON

ALFRED
HITCHCOCK

CHARLES DARWIN

THE SNOWMAN

M.C. ESCHER

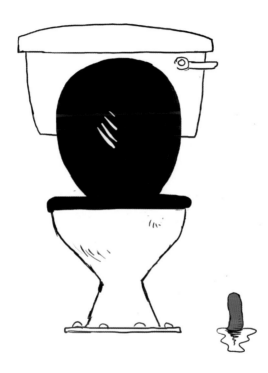

HOUDINI

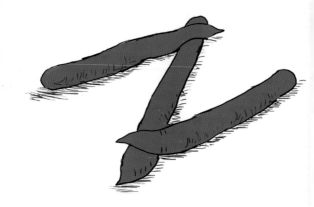

ZORRO